THIS JOURNAL BELONGS TO:

Spring unlocks the flowers to paint
the laughing soil.

REGINALD HEBER

I expect some new phases of life this summer,
and shall try to get the honey from each moment.

LUCY STONE

You don't have to light all the world,
but you do have to light your part.

It is only by forgetting yourself
that you draw near to God.

HENRY DAVID THOREAU

Better one true friend
than a hundred acquaintances.

EARLY AMERICAN PROVERB

We do not know how cheap the seeds of Happiness
are, or we should scatter them oftener.

Jᴀᴍᴇs Rᴜssᴇʟʟ Lᴏᴡᴇʟʟ

A heart at peace gives life to the body.

PROVERBS 14:30

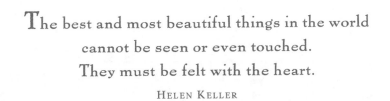

The best and most beautiful things in the world
cannot be seen or even touched.
They must be felt with the heart.

HELEN KELLER

The joy that you give to others
Is the joy that comes back to you.

JOHN GREENLEAF WHITTIER

_____

_____

_____

_____

_____

_____

_____

_____

_____

_____

_____

_____

_____

_____

_____

_____

_____

_____

_____

Hands to work,
Hearts to God

EARLY SHAKER MOTTO

Great beauty, great strength,
and great riches are really and truly no great use;
a right heart exceeds all.

BENJAMIN FRANKLIN

_____

_____

_____

_____

_____

_____

_____

_____

_____

_____

_____

_____

_____

_____

_____

_____

_____

There are three things that grow more precious
with age: old wood to burn, old books to read,
and old friends to enjoy.

I never spoke with God,
Nor visited in heaven ;
Yet certain am I of the spot
As if the chart were given.

EMILY DICKINSON

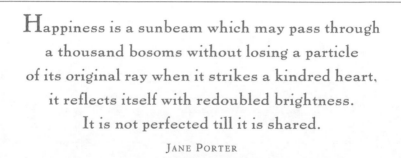

Happiness is a sunbeam which may pass through
a thousand bosoms without losing a particle
of its original ray when it strikes a kindred heart,
it reflects itself with redoubled brightness.
It is not perfected till it is shared.

Jane Porter

Give what you have. To someone
it may be better than you dare think.

HENRY WADSWORTH LONGFELLOW

Fill me with joy in your presence.

PSALM 16:11

I find as I grow older that
I love those most whom I loved first.

THOMAS JEFFERSON

He who lives in hope dances without a fiddle.

EARLY AMERICAN PROVERB

There never was any heart truly great and generous,
that was not also tender and compassionate.

ROBERT FROST

Bless our home, our lives, our friends
With love, that Lord, on Thee depends.

TRADITIONAL HOUSE BLESSING

The only thing that makes one place
more attractive to me than another is
the quantity of heart I find in it.

JANE WELSH CARLYLE

Heaven does not make holiness,
but holiness makes heaven.

EARLY AMERICAN PROVERB

Remember the day's blessings;
forget the day's troubles.

EARLY AMERICAN PROVERB

_____

_____

_____

_____

_____

_____

_____

_____

_____

_____

_____

_____

_____

_____

_____

_____

_____

_____

_____

When so rich a harvest is before us, why do we not
gather it? All is in our hands if we will but use it.

ELIZABETH SETON

Hurt not the earth, neither the sea, nor the trees.

REVELATION 7:3

I will be the gladdest thing under the sun,
I will touch a hundred flowers and not pick one.

EDNA ST. VINCENT MILLAY

Lord of the far horizons,
Give us the eyes to see
Over the verge of the sundown
The beauty that is to be.

BLISS CARMAN

The sunshine smiles upon the winter days of my heart, never doubting of its spring flowers.

RABINDRANATH TAGORE

All are needed by each one;
Nothing is fair or good alone.

RALPH WALDO EMERSON

_____

_____

_____

_____

_____

_____

_____

_____

_____

_____

_____

_____

_____

_____

_____

_____

_____

_____

_____

_____